As Expounded by Dada Bhagwan

The Essence of All Religion

Originally compiled in Gujarati :
Dr. Niruben Amin

Publisher	: **Mr. Ajit C. Patel**
Dada Bhagwan Vignan Foundation
1, Varun Apartment, 37, Shrimali Society,
Opp. Navrangpura Police Station,
Navrangpura, Ahmedabad: 380009.
Gujarat, India.
Tel. : +91 79 35002100, +91 9328661166-77
©	**Dada Bhagwan Foundation**
5, Mamta Park Society, B\h. Navgujarat College,
Usmanpura, Ahmedabad - 380014, Gujarat, India.
Email: info@dadabhagwan.org Tel.: +91 9328661166-77
All Rights Reserved. No part of this publication may be shared, copied, translated or reproduced in any form (including electronic storage or audio recording) without written permission from the holder of the copyright.
This publication is licensed for your personal use only.

1st Edition	: 2,000 copies,	April 2000
2nd to		
9th Edition	: 27,400 copies,	January 2001 to June 2019
10th Edition	: 3,000 copies,	April 2022

Price	: Ultimate humility and the intent that 'I do not know anything'!
Rs. 20.00
Printer	: **Amba Multiprint**
B - 99, Electronics GIDC, K-6 Road,
Sector - 25, Gandhinagar-382044.
Gujarat, India.
Tel. : +91 79 35002142, +91 9328660055

ISBN/eISBN : 978-93-85912-83-2

Printed in India

Trimantra

The Three Mantras That Destroy All Obstacles in Life

Namo Vitaraagaya

I bow to the Ones who are absolutely free from all attachment and abhorrence

Namo Arihantanam

I bow to the living Ones who have annihilated all internal enemies of anger, pride, deceit and greed

Namo Siddhanam

I bow to the Ones who have attained the state of total and final liberation

Namo Aayariyanam

I bow to the Self-realized masters who impart the Knowledge of the Self to others

Namo Uvazzayanam

I bow to the Ones who have received the Knowledge of the Self and are helping others attain the same

Namo Loye Savva Sahunam

I bow to the Ones, wherever they may be, who have received the Knowledge of the Self

Eso Pancha Namukkaro

These five salutations

Savva Pavappanasano

Destroy all demerit karma

Mangalanam Cha Savvesim

Of all that is auspicious

Padhamam Havai Mangalam ‖1‖

This is the highest

Om Namo Bhagavate Vasudevaya ‖2‖

I bow to the Ones who have attained the absolute Self in human form

Om Namah Shivaya ‖3‖

I bow to all human beings who have become instruments for the salvation of the world

Jai Sat Chit Anand

Awareness of the Eternal is Bliss

Books of Akram Vignan of Dada Bhagwan

1. Adjust Everywhere
2. Anger
3. Aptavani - 1
4. Aptavani - 2
5. Aptavani - 4
6. Aptavani - 5
7. Aptavani - 6
8. Aptavani - 8
9. Aptavani - 9
10. Autobiography of Gnani Purush A.M.Patel
11. Avoid Clashes
12. Brahmacharya: Celibacy Attained With Understanding
13. Death: Before, During and After...
14. Flawless Vision
15. Generation Gap
16. Harmony in Marriage
17. Life Without Conflict
18. Money
19. Noble Use of Money
20. Non-Violence
21. Pratikraman: The Master Key That Resolves All Conflicts (Abridged & Big Volume)
22. Pure Love
23. Right Understanding to Help Others
24. Science of Karma
25. Science of Speech
26. The Current Living Tirthankara Shree Simandhar Swami
27. Simple and Effective Science for Self-Realization
28. The Essence of All Religion
29. The Fault Is of the Sufferer
30. The Guru and the Disciple
31. The Hidden Meaning of Truth and Untruth
32. The Practice of Humanity
33. Trimantra
34. Whatever Has Happened Is Justice
35. Who Am I?
36. Worries

'Dadavani' Magazine is published every month in English

Who Is Dada Bhagwan?

In June 1958, around 6 o'clock one evening, amidst the hustle and bustle of the Surat railway station while seated on a bench, 'Dada Bhagwan' manifested completely within the sacred bodily form of Ambalal Muljibhai Patel. Nature revealed a remarkable phenomenon of spirituality! In the span of an hour, the vision of the universe was unveiled to him! Complete clarity for all spiritual questions such as, 'Who are we? Who is God? Who runs the world? What is karma? What is liberation?' etc. was attained.

What He attained that evening, He imparted to others through his original Scientific experiment (*Gnan Vidhi*) in just two hours! This has been referred to as the *Akram* path. *Kram* means to climb up sequentially, step-by-step while *Akram* means step-less, a shortcut, the elevator path!

He, himself, would explain to others who Dada Bhagwan is by saying, "The one visible before you is not Dada Bhagwan. I am the *Gnani Purush* and the One who has manifested within is Dada Bhagwan who is the Lord of the fourteen worlds. He is also within you, and within everyone else too. He resides unmanifest within you, whereas here [within A. M. Patel], He has manifested completely! I, myself, am not God (*Bhagwan*); I also bow down to the Dada Bhagwan who has manifest within me."

❖ ❖ ❖ ❖ ❖

The Current Link to Attain Self-Realization

After attaining the Knowledge of the Self in 1958, absolutely revered Dada Bhagwan (Dadashri) traveled nationally and internationally to impart spiritual discourse and Self-realization to spiritual seekers.

During his lifetime itself, Dadashri had given the spiritual power to Pujya Dr. Niruben Amin (Niruma) to bestow Self-realization to others. In the same way, after Dadashri left his mortal body, Pujya Niruma conducted spiritual discourses (*satsang*) and imparted Self-realization to spiritual seekers, as an instrumental doer. Dadashri had also given Pujya Deepakbhai Desai the spiritual power to conduct *satsang*. At present, with the blessings of Pujya Niruma, Pujya Deepakbhai travels nationally and internationally to impart Self-realization as an instrumental doer.

After Self-realization, thousands of spiritual seekers prevail in a state free from bondage and dwell in the experience of the Self, whilst carrying out all their worldly responsibilities.

❖ ❖ ❖ ❖ ❖

Note About This Translation

The *Gnani Purush*, Ambalal M. Patel, also commonly known as 'Dadashri' or 'Dada', gave spiritual discourses that were in the form of answers to questions asked by spiritual aspirants. These discourses were recorded and compiled into books by Pujya Dr. Niruben Amin in the Gujarati language.

Dadashri had said that it would be impossible to translate His *satsangs* and the Knowledge about the Science of Self-realization word for word into other languages, because some of the meaning would be lost in the process. Therefore, in order to understand precisely the *Akram* Science of Self-realization, He stressed the importance of learning Gujarati.

However, Dadashri did grant His blessings to translate His words into other languages so that spiritual seekers could benefit to a certain degree and later progress through their own efforts. This book is not a literal translation, but great care has been taken to preserve the essence of His original message.

Spiritual discourses have been and continue to be translated from Gujarati. For certain Gujarati words, several translated words or even sentences are needed to convey the meaning, hence many Gujarati words have been retained within the translated text for better understanding. Where the Gujarati word is used for the first time, it is italicized, followed by a translation explaining its meaning in parenthesis. Subsequently, only the Gujarati word is used in the text that follows. This serves a two-fold benefit; firstly, ease of translation and reading, and secondly, make the reader more familiar with the Gujarati words, which is critical for a deeper understanding of this spiritual Science. The content in square brackets provides further clarity regarding the matter, which is not present in the original Gujarati content.

This is a humble attempt to present to the world, the essence of His Knowledge. While reading this translation, if there is any contradiction or discrepancy, then it is the mistake of the translators and the understanding of the matter should be clarified with the living *Gnani* to avoid misinterpretation.

❖ ❖ ❖ ❖ ❖

Special Note to the Reader

The Self is the Soul (*Atma*) within all living beings.

The term pure Soul is used by the *Gnani Purush* for the awakened Self, after the *Gnan Vidhi*. The word Self, with an uppercase 'S', refers to the awakened Self which is separate from the worldly-interacting self, which is written with a lowercase 's'.

Wherever Dadashri uses the term 'we', 'us', or 'our', He is referring to Himself, the *Gnani Purush*.

Similarly, the use of You or Your in the middle of a sentence, with an uppercase first letter, or 'You', 'Your' in single quotes at the beginning of the sentence, refers to the state of the awakened Self or *Pragnya*. This is an important distinction for the correct understanding of the difference between the awakened Self and the worldly-interacting self.

Wherever the name 'Chandubhai' is used, the reader should substitute his or her name and read the matter accordingly.

The masculine third person pronoun 'he' and likewise the object pronoun 'him' have been used for the most part throughout the translation. Needless to say, 'he' includes 'she' and 'him' includes 'her'.

For reference, a glossary of all the Gujarati words is either provided at the back of this book or available on our website at:

http://www.dadabhagwan.org/books-media/glossary/

❖ ❖ ❖ ❖ ❖

Editorial

All throughout the day, whether at home, in the midst of worldly interactions or elsewhere, we keep hearing from people, "I do not want to do this, yet it ends up happening! I want to do this, yet I am not able to! I have a strong intention (*bhaavna*). I have a very strong, firm resolve to do it, and the efforts are there too, yet I am not able to do it!"

The perpetual complaint of every religious instructor for his or her spiritual aspirant is, "You are not digesting what we are saying." Those listening to the discourses also become perplexed and discouraged [wondering], 'Despite carrying out all these religious practices, why does my behavior not change?' What is the reason behind this? Where is the obstruction? In what way can one overcome the mistake that is being made?

Absolutely revered Dadashri recognized the limitations of the human beings of this age and provided them with a suitable answer using an entirely novel and completely scientific approach. Revered Dadashri gave the scientific explanation that conduct is a result, it is an effect, whereas intent (*bhaav*) is a cause. It is not possible to directly bring about a change in that which is an effect. That too can only be done through a scientific approach. If the cause changes, then the effect will change on its own! To change the cause, start anew in this life and change the intent. To change the intent, Dadashri has taught us to nurture the Nine *Kalams*. That which all the scriptures inculcate yet does not bear result, Dadashri has given in the form of keys through the Nine *Kalams*, to bring about a change from the root level. By following this, hundreds of thousands of people have improved not just this life but all lives from here on! Truly speaking, an external change may not come forth in this life, but by nurturing the intentions of these Nine *Kalams*, the new causes within change entirely, and tremendous inner peace prevails! One stops seeing faults in others, and that becomes the primary cause for bringing about eternal peace! And in that too, many people have nurtured intentions similar to that of the Nine *Kalams* in the past life, and so in this life, that indeed comes into effect in the form of this very link, thus bringing about a change in the conduct, immediately, right now!

To attain any sort of spiritual power (*siddhi*) [that is presently lacking within], all that needs to be done is to keep asking for the energies from the God within. That will definitely bear result.

Absolutely revered Dadashri said about himself, "I have been practicing these Nine *Kalams* my entire life; they are in fact my wealth. So, I have disclosed my daily practices, ultimately for the sake of the salvation of the public. These Nine *Kalams* have been going on within daily, constantly, for so many years, for the past forty years. I have presented this to the public."

For many spiritual aspirants, the belief becomes firm within that, 'I know everything similar to that which is contained in these Nine *Kalams* and it prevails exactly like that for me.' But when we ask them, "Do you hurt other people?" If we ask their family members or those close to them, then they will say, "Yes." This means that they have not known this in the correct sense. What they have known will not be useful. In that case, if that which the *Gnani Purush* has accomplished in his own life is shared through the medium of His experience-laden speech, then it will be effective. Therefore, the intention should be in accordance with the design provided by the *Gnani Purush*; only then will it be of use and lead to speedy progress on the path to liberation! And ultimately, it will bear result to such a point that no living being will be hurt in the slightest extent! Not only that, but by nurturing the intentions of the Nine *Kalams* daily, so many faults get washed off! And one is able to progress further on the path to liberation!

Dr. Niruben Amin

The Essence of All Religion

(The Nine Kalams: The Essence of All the Scriptures)

All Obstacles Are Destroyed Through the Nine Kalams

Dadashri: I am giving you a book to read. I am not giving you big books to read. Just a small one for you. Just say this much, just this much.

Questioner: That is fine.

Dadashri: Just read this once! Read the entire thing. This is a 'medicine' that I am giving you, it is a 'medicine' that is to be read. These Nine *Kalams* are only to be read; this is not a 'medicine' that requires 'doing'. Besides, whatever you are doing is correct, but this is a 'medicine' that calls for nurturing the intention (*bhaavna*). Therefore, keep reading what 'we' are giving you. All kinds of obstacles will break through them.

So, first take a minute or two and read these Nine *Kalams*.

Questioner: The Nine *Kalams*...

1. Oh Dada Bhagwan, give me the absolute energy not to hurt, cause anyone to hurt, nor instigate anyone to hurt the ego of any living being, even to the slightest extent.

   Give me the absolute energy not to hurt, even to the slightest extent, the ego of any living being, and to conduct my thoughts, speech, and action in a manner that is accepted by all.

   He Dada Bhagwan! Mane koi pan dehadhaari jeevatma no kinchitmaatra pan aham na dubhay, na dubhavay, ke dubhavava pratye na anumoday evi param shakti aapo.

   Mane koi pan dehadhaari jeevatma no kinchitmaatra pan aham na dubhay evi syadvaad vani, syadvaad vartan ane syadvaad manan karvani param shakti aapo.

2. Oh Dada Bhagwan, give me the absolute energy not to hurt, cause anyone to hurt, nor instigate anyone to hurt the foundation of any religion, even to the slightest extent.

   Give me the absolute energy not to hurt, even to the slightest extent, the foundation of any religion and to conduct my thoughts, speech, and action in a manner that is accepted by all.

   He Dada Bhagwan! Mane koi pan dharma nu kinchitmaatra pan pramaan na dubhay, na dubhavay, ke dubhavava pratye na anumoday evi param shakti aapo.

   Mane koi pan dharma nu kinchitmaatra pan pramaan na dubhavay evi syadvaad vani, syadvaad vartan ane syadvaad manan karvani param shakti aapo.

3. Oh Dada Bhagwan, give me the absolute energy not to criticize, offend, or disrespect any living preacher, monk, nun, or religious head.

He Dada Bhagwan! Mane koi pan dehadhaari updeshak, sadhu, sadhvi, ke aacharya no avarnavaad, aparaadh, avinay na karvani param shakti aapo.

4. Oh Dada Bhagwan, give me the absolute energy not to, nor cause anyone to, nor instigate anyone to, dislike or have contempt for any living being, even to the slightest extent.

   He Dada Bhagwan! Mane koi pan dehadhaari jeevatma pratye kinchitmaatra pan abhaav, tiraskaar kyaarey pan na karaay, na karaavaay ke karta pratye na anumoday evi param shakti aapo.

5. Oh Dada Bhagwan, give me the absolute energy not to, nor cause anyone to, nor instigate anyone to speak any harsh or hurtful language towards any living being, even to the slightest extent.

   If someone speaks any harsh or hurtful language, give me the energy to speak kindly and softly in reply.

   He Dada Bhagwan! Mane koi pan dehadhaari jeevatma saathe kyaarey pan kathor bhaasha, tanteeli bhaasha na bolay, na bolavay, ke bolva pratye na anumoday evi param shakti aapo.

   Koi kathor bhaasha, tanteeli bhaasha bole to mane mrudu-ruju bhaasha bolvani shaktio aapo.

6. Oh Dada Bhagwan, give me the absolute energy not to have, nor cause anyone to have, nor instigate anyone to have, even to the slightest extent, any sexual faults, desires, gestures, or faults related to sexual thoughts towards any living being, be it male, female, or of bisexual orientation.

   Give me the absolute energy to be continuously free from all sexual impulses.

   He Dada Bhagwan! Mane koi pan dehadhaari jeevatma

pratye stri, purush agar napunsak, gamme te lingadhari hoi, to tena sambandhi kinchitmaatra pan vishay-vikaar sambandhi dosho, ichchhao, cheshtao ke vichaar sambandhi dosho na karaay, na karaavaay ke karta pratye na anumoday evi param shakti aapo.

Mane nirantar nirvikaar rahevani param shakti aapo.

7. Oh Dada Bhagwan, give me the energy to not have excessive temptation towards any particular food taste.

   Give me the absolute energy to take meals with a balance of all tastes.

   He Dada Bhagwan! Mane koi pan ras ma lubdhapanu na karaay evi shakti aapo.

   Samrasi khoraak levaay evi param shakti aapo.

8. Oh Dada Bhagwan, give me the absolute energy not to, nor cause anyone to, nor instigate anyone to criticize, offend, or disrespect any being, be they present or absent, living or dead.

   He Dada Bhagwan! Mane koi pan dehadhaari jeevatma no pratyaksh agar paroksh, jeevant agar mrutyu paamelano, koi no kinchitmaatra pan avarnavaad, aparaadh, avinay na karaay, na karaavaay ke karta pratye na anumoday evi param shakti aapo.

9. Oh Dada Bhagwan, give me the absolute energy to become an instrument for the salvation of the world.

   He Dada Bhagwan! Mane jagat kalyan karvaanu nimit banvaani param shakti aapo, shakti aapo, shakti aapo.

   (Read these three times a day.)

You should ask this much from 'Dada Bhagwan' [the Lord within]. This is not something that is to be recited daily, it is something that should remain in your heart. This is something that should be nurtured daily, with applied awareness. The essence of all the scriptures is encompassed in this much text.

Dadashri: Did you read it word for word?

Questioner: Yes, sir. I have read everything carefully.

To Not Hurt Anyone's Ego...

Questioner: Please explain the meaning of the first *Kalam*:

"Oh Dada Bhagwan, give me the absolute energy not to hurt, cause anyone to hurt, nor instigate anyone to hurt the ego of any living being, even to the slightest extent.

Give me the absolute energy not to hurt, even to the slightest extent, the ego of any living being, and to conduct my thoughts, speech, and action in a manner that is accepted by all."

Dadashri: We are asking for *syadvaad vani* (speech that is accepted by all) so that no one's ego is hurt. Such speech will come forth for you gradually. The speech that I am speaking is verily the result I have obtained by nurturing these very intentions.

Questioner: But in this, although no one's ego should be hurt, it doesn't mean that I should support someone's ego, does it?

Dadashri: No, you are not to support the ego. Rather, the ego should not be hurt. What I am saying is, do not break the 'glasses'. That does not mean that you should protect the 'glasses'. They already lie protected. Therefore, do not break them. Then they will remain in their protected state by default. You should not become instrumental (a *nimit*) in breaking them. If they are breaking, then do not become instrumental in breaking them. And you are to nurture the intention, 'May no living being be hurt through me, may no one's ego be shattered.' Maintain this much. Consider the other person to be beneficial.

Questioner: In business, it is not always the case that the other person's ego is not hurt. I constantly end up hurting the ego of one person or another.

Dadashri: That is not considered hurting someone's ego. The ego is hurt for instance, when a person tries to speak, and you say, "That's enough, that's enough. You are not to speak." Do not hurt his ego in this way. Whereas in business, it is not actually the ego that is hurt, it is the mind that is hurt.

Questioner: But it's not as if the ego is a good thing, right? So then, what is the problem in hurting it?

Dadashri: He himself currently [believes he] is the ego, therefore you should not hurt it. He himself is all of that. In whatever he does, he believes, 'I am indeed this.' Therefore, you should not hurt it. That is why you should not scold anyone, not even the family members. You should make sure that no one's ego is hurt. No one's ego should be hurt. If a person's ego is hurt, then he becomes estranged from you. Thereafter, he will not come close to you again. You should never say to someone, "You are useless, you are like this, you are like that." You should not belittle anyone like that. Yes, you may scold him. There is no objection to scolding him, but in whichever way possible, the ego should not be hurt. There is no problem if he gets hit on the head, as long as his ego is not hurt. You should not shatter anyone's ego.

And you should not have contempt for anyone, not even the house-help. Contempt hurts his ego. If you do not need his services, then tell him gently, "I do not need your services," and if it does not hurt his ego, then you can even let him go by giving him some money [as settlement]. The money will be recovered, but his ego should not be hurt. Otherwise, he will bind vengeance; he will bind tremendous vengeance! He will not allow you to progress [spiritually], he will come in the way.

This is actually a very subtle point. Nevertheless, if you happen to hurt someone's ego, then you should ask for the energy [in accordance with this *Kalam*] from 'us' [the Lord within]. Therefore, because one maintains an opinion that differs from whatever has happened, there is not much liability for that. This is because one's opinion has now changed. By asking for this [energy as per the first *Kalam*], the opinion that was previously there of hurting someone's ego has now become different [from the action].

Questioner: What does it mean 'to have become separate from the opinion'?

Dadashri: 'Dada Bhagwan' [the Lord within] has understood, 'Now, this poor fellow ['Chandubhai'] no longer has the intention of hurting anyone's ego.' You do not have the desire to hurt anyone, yet this ends up happening. Whereas for the people of the world [who are not Self-realized], it ends up happening in concordance with their desire. Therefore, by saying this *Kalam,* your opinion becomes different [from the action]. Therefore, you have become free from that context.

Therefore, all you have to do is ask for the energy (*shakti*). You do not have to do anything else; you just have to ask for the energy. This does not need to be put into application.

Questioner: Asking for the energy is fine, but what should we do so that the other person's ego is not hurt?

Dadashri: No, you do not have to do anything like that. You just have to ask [for the energy] as per this *Kalam*; that is all. Nothing else has to be done. Right now, when someone's ego ends up being hurt, it is an effect that has already come [into discharge]. That which has happened now had already been decided, and it is not possible to stop it either. To try to change that is just a headache. But if you say this [*Kalam*], then the liability no longer remains.

Questioner: And it should be spoken genuinely, with a true heart.

Dadashri: Actually, everything should be done genuinely, with a true heart. And whoever speaks this [*Kalam*], does not do so insincerely, he indeed does it genuinely. But in this, your opinion has now become different [from the action]; this is the most ultimate science of a kind.

You do not have to act in accordance with the Nine *Kalams*, you simply have to say them. You simply have to ask for the energy, "Dada Bhagwan, give me the energy. I want this energy." So, you will attain that energy and the liability will cease. Whereas, what kind of knowledge does the world teach you? "Do not do this." Oh brother, I do not want to do it, but it ends up happening. That is why your knowledge does not fit with me. This approach fails to stop things from happening in the future and it also fails to prevent them from happening right now; both get spoiled. Therefore, the approach should be one that fits.

Bhaav Pratikraman, on the Moment

Questioner: When the other person's ego is hurt, at that time I realize that it is my own ego that has spoken.

Dadashri: No, there is no need to come to that conclusion. What does our awareness (*jagruti*) tell us? Our path to liberation is a path of introspection! Constantly remain in the inner awareness, and if the other person's ego is hurt, then immediately do *pratikraman* (exact method of reversal from aggression through confession of a mistake, apology, and resolution not to repeat the mistake) for it; that is our job. You already do so much *pratikraman*, this is one more to do! If I ever end up hurting anyone's ego, then I also do *pratikraman*.

Therefore, early in the morning say, "May no living being in this world be hurt, even to the slightest extent, through the mind, speech, and body." Say this five times and then get on with your day. And thereafter, whatever hurt is given, it has happened against your desire. Do *pratikraman* for that in the evening.

What is *pratikraman*? It is like washing off a stain the moment it occurs. Thereafter, there is no problem. Is there any problem thereafter? Who would not do *pratikraman*? Those people who are in a state of gross unawareness do not do *pratikraman*. Otherwise, those to whom I have given *Gnan* (Knowledge of the Self), how have those people become? They have become astute people. They think things through from moment to moment. The followers of the twenty-two *Tirthankars* were astute; they would only do shoot-on-sight *pratikraman*. They would 'shoot' [do *pratikraman*] as soon as a mistake arose! Whereas people of today cannot do that, so Lord Mahavir laid down these *raishi*, *devshi*, *pakshik*, and *samvatsari pratikraman* (*pratikraman* done in the morning, in the evening, every fortnight, and once a year, respectively).

Thoughts, Speech, and Action, Accepted by All...

Questioner: "Give me the absolute energy not to hurt, even to the slightest extent, the ego of any living being, and to conduct my thoughts, speech, and action in a manner that is accepted by all (*syadvaad*)." Please explain this.

Dadashri: *Syadvaad* means to know through which intent (*bhaav*), through which viewpoint, a person is speaking.

Questioner: To understand the other person's viewpoint, does that count as *syadvaad*?

Dadashri: To understand the other person's viewpoint, and to interact with him accordingly, that is referred to as *syadvaad*. Carry out worldly interactions such that the other person's viewpoint is not hurt. When you speak in a way that the viewpoint of a thief is not hurt, that is referred to as *syadvaad*!

When I speak here, whether the person is a Muslim or a Parsi, they all understand equally. The foundation of no one's belief system (*pramaan*) should be hurt, [by saying things like,] "Parsis are like this, or the *Sthanakvasis* (name of a Jain sect) are like this." No one should be hurt in this way.

Questioner: If there is a thief sitting amongst us, and we say, "It is not good to steal," then his mind is bound to be hurt, is it not?

Dadashri: No, you should not speak like that. You should tell the person, "This is the consequence of stealing. If you think it is appropriate, then do it." That is how you should speak. Hence, the matter should be conveyed methodically, then the other person may even be willing to listen. Otherwise, the person will not listen to that at all, and on the contrary, your words will be wasted. The words you have spoken will be in vain, and instead, the person will bind vengeance [thinking], 'Who is he to tell me!' That is not how it should be.

People say that it is an offence to steal, but the thief believes, 'It is my *dharma* (religion) to steal.' If someone were to bring a thief to me, then I would put my arm around his shoulder and ask him in private, "Brother, do you like this business? Do you enjoy it?" Then he would tell me the entire truth about himself. He would not feel fear in my presence. It is out of fear that people lie. Then I would explain to him, "Do you know the liability that goes with what you are doing? Are you aware of the consequences of such action?" And [the opinion], 'You are stealing,' does not even exist in my mind. If that were ever in my mind, then it would have an effect on him. Every person is in his own *dharma* (religion; function). To not hurt the foundation of any religion is considered *syadvaad* speech. *Syadvaad* speech is complete (*sampurna*). Each person's *prakruti* (mind-speech-body complex) is different, yet *syadvaad* speech does not object to anyone's *prakruti*.

Questioner: What does *syadvaad manan* mean?

Dadashri: *Syadvaad manan* means that even in thoughts, even in thinking, the foundation of any religion should not be hurt. It should definitely not be in the conduct, but it should also not be in the thoughts. Not only in what is spoken externally, but also in the mind, there should be good thoughts, such that the foundation of the other person's belief system is not hurt. This is because the thoughts that are in the mind reach the other person. That is indeed why these people's faces look disgruntled. Because your thoughts reach there and have an effect.

Questioner: Should we do *pratikraman* if a bad thought arises for someone?

Dadashri: Yes, otherwise the other person's mind will become disturbed. And when you do *pratikraman*, then even if his mind is disturbed, it will calm down. You should not think negatively or anything along those lines, for anyone. Everyone should look out for themselves; that is all. There are no other concerns.

To Not Hurt the Foundation of Any Belief System...

Questioner: The second *Kalam*. "Oh Dada Bhagwan, give me the absolute energy not to hurt, cause anyone to hurt, nor instigate anyone to hurt the foundation of any religion, even to the slightest extent. Give me the absolute energy not to hurt, even to the slightest extent, the foundation of any religion and to conduct my thoughts, speech, and action in a manner that is accepted by all."

Dadashri: The foundation of no one's belief system should be hurt. You should not feel that anyone is wrong. Does 'one' also not count as a figure?

Questioner: Yes.

Dadashri: Then does 'two' count as a figure?

Questioner: Yes, it does.

Dadashri: And what do those who are at '100' say? "Ours is correct, yours is wrong." That should not be said. Everyone's [religion] is correct. 'One' is correct at its level, 'two' at its level, they are all correct according to their level. Therefore, that which accepts each and every level, is called *syadvaad*. Say a certain thing is in its intrinsic functional properties, but if we accept only some of its properties and reject others, then that is wrong. *Syadvaad* means to accept the foundation of each person's belief system. If one is at 360 degrees, then [he sees that] everyone is correct, however [he knows that] this person is correct up to his degree, and the other person is correct up to his degree.

Therefore, we cannot say that Islam is wrong. Every religion is correct, it is not wrong. We cannot say that anybody is wrong! That is his religion. How can we tell someone who eats meat that he is wrong? He will say, "It is part of my religion to eat meat." Therefore, we cannot negate it. That is his belief. We cannot crush anyone's belief. However, if our own people are eating meat, then we should tell them, "Brother, this is not a good thing." Thereafter, if he still wants to do it, then we cannot object to it. We should explain to him that this is not a beneficial thing.

Syadvaad means the foundation of the belief system of any religion is not hurt. However much truth there is to it, it refers to that much as the truth, and however much is false, it even refers to that much as false. That is considered as not hurting the foundation of the belief system. The foundation of the belief system of Christians, of Muslims, the foundation of the belief system of any religion should not be hurt. This is because they are all contained within 360 degrees. Real is the center and all these others are relative views. For the one at the center, the relative views are all equal. The *syadvaad* of God means that no one is hurt in the slightest extent, no matter which religion he follows!

Therefore, this is what the *syadvaad* path is like. Everyone's religion must be accepted. Even if the other person slaps you twice, you should accept it; because the entire world is flawless. You see others as being at fault due to your own faults. Besides, the world is not at fault whatsoever, whereas your intellect shows people to be at fault [by deeming], 'This person did wrong.'

Criticize, Offend, Disrespect...

Questioner: What is the exact meaning of the word *avarnavaad* in the third *Kalam*? "Oh Dada Bhagwan, give me the absolute energy not to criticize, offend, or disrespect any living preacher, monk, nun, or religious head."

Dadashri: To not depict something as it is by any means possible, but to depict the opposite, that is *avarnavaad*! Not only is it not as it is, but it is actually the opposite of that. To depict something as it is, and to refer to the bad [part] as bad and to refer to the good [part] as good, that is not considered *avarnavaad*. But when everything that is said is untrue, that is when it is considered *avarnavaad*. Is there not some good in every person? And there may be some bad as well. But if you speak only negatively about him, that is when it is considered *avarnavaad*. You should say, "He lacks a little in this matter, but in these other matters he is very good!"

Avarnavaad means you know about a person, you know certain things about him, yet you speak contrary to the facts, you talk about qualities he does not possess. To talk about qualities that he does not possess is all *avarnavaad*. *Varnavaad* means to say something as it is, and *avarnavaad* is to say that which is not fact. That is considered a huge *viradhana*, the greatest *viradhana* (to speak that which is contrary to fact about a person, leading to spiritual descent). When it is done for others, common people, it is considered backbiting (*ninda*), but when it is done for elevated people, it is considered *avarnavaad*. Elevated people refers to those who are progressing spiritually. Elevated people does not refer to those who are in high posts in worldly interactions, it does not refer to presidents; it is referred to as *avarnavaad* when it is done for those who are progressing spiritually. That is a grave liability! *Avarnavaad* is a grave liability! It is worse than *viradhana*.

Questioner: That includes preachers, monks, and heads of religious orders, doesn't it?

Dadashri: Yes, all of them. It does not matter if they are on the right path or not, whether they are Self-realized or not, that is not for you to see. After all, are they not followers of Lord Mahavir? Whatever they are doing, they are doing it in Lord Mahavir's name, aren't they? Whatever they do, whether right or wrong, they are doing it in Lord

Mahavir's name, aren't they? Therefore, you cannot speak falsely about them (*avarnavaad*).

Questioner: What is the difference between *avarnavaad* and *viradhana*?

Dadashri: With *viradhana*, one goes in the wrong direction, descends, goes to a lower life-form (*gati*). Whereas with *avarnavaad*, if one does *pratikraman* for it thereafter, then there is no problem, it becomes regular [goes back to normal]. If you speak falsely about someone, but you do *pratikraman* for it afterwards, then it gets cleared off.

Questioner: Please explain a little more about *avinay* and *viradhana*.

Dadashri: *Avinay* is not considered *viradhana*. *Avinay* is a step lower, whereas in *viradhana* the person purposefully opposes another. *Avinay* is the attitude of, 'It does not concern me.' To not give respect, that is considered *avinay*.

Questioner: What is *aparaadh*?

Dadashri: If a person does *aaradhana* (worships devotedly), then he rises higher, and if he does *viradhana*, then he descends. But the one who does *aparaadh* (commits an offence) takes a beating from both sides. A person who does *aparaadh* does not progress himself, nor does he let anyone else progress. Such a person is referred to as an *aparaadhi*.

Questioner: Even in *viradhana*, one does not allow others to progress, right?

Dadashri: But comparatively, the person who does *viradhana* is better. If someone were to find out, they may show him the right direction by telling him, "On what basis did you say that? How can what you say be true!" Then he may even turn around. But an *aparaadhi* will neither turn around nor advance. The one who does *viradhana* may walk in the wrong direction, but he will fall down!

Questioner: But is there a chance for the one who does *viradhana* to turn around?

Dadashri: Yes, there is definitely a chance to turn back around!

Questioner: Is there a chance to turn back around for the *aparaadhi*?

Dadashri: He neither turns around nor does he make any progress. He has no inclination. He does not move forward, nor does he move backward. Whenever you see him, he remains exactly where he was; that is referred to as *aparaadh*.

Questioner: What is the definition of *aparaadh*?

Dadashri: *Viradhana* occurs without the desire for it and *aparaadh* occurs with the desire.

Questioner: How does that happen, Dada?

Dadashri: If a person becomes obstinate, then he may end up committing an offence (*aparaadh*). When one does *viradhana* despite knowing that he should not, that falls under *aparaadh*. The one who does *viradhana* may be released, but the one that does *aparaadh* will not be released. A person with a very tremendous, strong ego will end up doing *aparaadh*. This is why you should tell yourself, 'You are a fool. You are carrying yourself around pompously for no reason. People may not know it, but I know what you are like. You are crazy.' You have to come up with some kind of a solution. You have to do some plus and minus; if you only do multiplication, then where will it lead? Therefore, you should do some division. The total sum and the remainder after subtraction are subject to nature, whereas multiplication and division are in your hands. If this ego multiplies it by seven, then divide it by seven, so there is no remainder!

Questioner: When we backbite about someone, what does that fall under?

Dadashri: Backbiting (*ninda*) falls under *viradhana*, but it can be erased with *pratikraman*. It is like *avarnavaad*. That is why I say, "Do not backbite about anyone." Even then, people talk behind others' backs. Hey, you should not backbite. This environment is filled entirely with *parmanus* (the smallest, most indivisible and indestructible particles of matter). Everything [these vibrations] will reach the person being talked about. Not a single irresponsible word should be spoken about anyone. And if you must say something, then say something nice, say something respectable, do not say something disgraceful.

Therefore, do not become involved in backbiting about anyone. There is no problem if you cannot sing praises, but do not become involved in backbiting. What I am conveying is, 'What benefit do you get from backbiting?' There is tremendous loss in that. If there is tremendous loss in anything in this world, then it is in backbiting. Therefore, there should be no reason to backbite about anyone.

There is no such thing as backbiting here at all. We are merely discussing this to understand what is right and what is wrong! The Lord has said, "Know what is wrong as wrong and what is right as right. However, there should not be the slightest abhorrence towards that which one knows to be wrong, and there should not be the slightest attachment towards that which one knows to be right." If you do not know that which is wrong as wrong, then you will not be able to know that which is right as right. Therefore, we should discuss it in detail. Knowledge can be understood [exactly] only from the *Gnani*.

One Should Not Have Dislike, Contempt...

Questioner: The fourth *Kalam*. "Oh Dada Bhagwan, give me the absolute energy not to, nor cause anyone to, nor instigate anyone to, dislike or have contempt for any living being, even to the slightest extent."

Dadashri: Yes, that is correct. If you feel dislike towards someone, for example you are sitting in your office and someone walks in, you may feel a sense of dislike (*abhaav*) or contempt (*tiraskaar*) for that person. So you should think about it and feel remorseful, that it should not be this way.

One can never be free as long as he has contempt. Nothing but vengeance is bound through that. No matter whom you have contempt for, be it only towards inanimate objects, even then you will not become free. Therefore, the slightest of contempt for anyone will not do. And as long as you have contempt for anyone, you cannot become *vitaraag* (free from attachment and abhorrence). In fact, you will have to become *vitaraag*, only then can you become free!

One Should Not Speak Harsh, Hurtful Language...

Questioner: The fifth *Kalam*: "Oh Dada Bhagwan, give me the absolute energy not to, nor cause anyone to, nor instigate anyone to speak any harsh or hurtful language towards any living being, even to the slightest extent. If someone speaks any harsh or hurtful language, give me the energy to speak kindly and softly in reply."

Dadashri: You should not speak harsh language. If you end up speaking harsh language with someone and he feels hurt, then you should apologize to him in person [by saying], "Friend, I made a mistake, I am sorry, please forgive me." If you cannot tell him in person, then repent from within, 'I should not speak like this.'

Questioner: And we should remind ourselves repeatedly, to not speak like this.

Dadashri: Yes, you should think this over and repent over it. It will stop only if repentance is done. Otherwise, it will not stop automatically. It does not cease by simply saying [I'm sorry].

Questioner: What is *mrudu, ruju* language?

Dadashri: *Ruju* means it is straightforward and *mrudu* means it is with humility. When it [speech] is filled with utmost humility, it is considered *mrudu*. So you should speak language that is straightforward and is with humility and ask for the energy to do so. In doing so, that energy will arise. If you spoke harsh language and your son felt hurt, then you should repent over it. And you should also tell your son, "I am sorry, please forgive me. I will not speak in this way again." This is the only way to improve the speech and 'this' is the only college.

Questioner: So what is the difference between harsh and hurtful language, and language that is with humility and is straightforward?

Dadashri: Many people use harsh language like, "You are worthless, you are a crook, you are a thief." They use words that we may never have heard before! Upon hearing harsh words, our heart may even come to a stop. Such harsh speech is never considered pleasant. Rather, one may think, 'Where is this coming from!' Harsh speech is egotistical.

And what does *tantilli* language mean? There is contention while competing with someone, isn't there? "See how well I cooked. And she does not even know how to cook." In the same way, one becomes involved in contention, one starts to compete. This *tantilli* (hurtful) language is very bad.

Harsh and hurtful language should not be spoken. All the faults through speech are covered by these two words. So when you have spare time, you should keep asking Dada Bhagwan for energies. If you tend to speak unpleasantly, then ask for energy for the opposite; "Give me the energy to speak pure speech (*shuddha vani*). Give me the energy to speak speech that is accepted by all (*syadvaad vani*). Give me the energy to speak kindly and softly in reply. Keep asking for such [energy]. *Syadvaad vani* means speech that does not hurt anyone.

...Give Me the Energy to Remain Free From Sexual Impulses

Questioner: The sixth *Kalam*. "Oh Dada Bhagwan, give me the absolute energy not to have, nor cause anyone to have, nor instigate anyone to have, even to the slightest extent, any sexual faults, desires, gestures, or faults related to sexual thoughts towards any living being, be it male, female, or of bisexual orientation. Give me the absolute energy to be continuously free from all sexual impulses."

Dadashri: If you happen to view someone with a sexual intent, then immediately tell Chandubhai [reader to insert his or her name here], 'This is not right. This does not suit you. You are a person with noble qualities. Just as you have a sister, she may also be someone's sister! If someone were to view your sister with a sexual intent, then how hurt would you feel? Similarly, would someone else not feel hurt? Therefore, this does not suit you.' So, if you happen to view someone with a sexual intent, then repent over it.

Questioner: What does *cheshtao* mean?

Dadashri: Actions of the body that can be photographed are all considered *cheshtao*. If you are making fun of someone, that is considered *cheshta*. If you are laughing, that is considered *cheshta*.

Questioner: So when we make fun of someone, when we pull a prank on him, are those *cheshtao*?

Dadashri: There are many different kinds of *cheshtao*.

Questioner: What are the *cheshtao* related to sexuality like?

Dadashri: As all activities of the body pertaining to sexuality can be photographed, they are all *cheshtao*. That which cannot be done through the body are not *cheshtao*. Sometimes sexual desires and thoughts arise, but they do not come into action. Faults pertaining to thoughts are of the mind!

"Give me the absolute energy to be continuously free from all sexual impulses." You should ask for this much from Dada. Dada can bestow such grace!

Do Not Have Excessive Temptation in Any Taste...

Questioner: The seventh *Kalam*. "Oh Dada Bhagwan, give me the energy to not have excessive temptation towards any particular food taste. Give me the absolute energy to take meals with a balance of all tastes."

Dadashri: When you sit down to eat and you only like certain vegetable dishes, only those made with tomatoes, and you keep remembering them later on, that is considered as prevailing in excessive temptation (*lubdhapanu*). There is nothing wrong with eating tomatoes, but it should not keep coming to memory. Otherwise all of your energies will be drawn towards the prevalence in excessive temptation. Therefore, you should say, "Whatever is served is fine with me." There should not be a prevalence in excessive temptation of any kind. Whatever is served on your plate, eat it without further ado. There should be no objection to it. Instead, accept whatever is served on your plate. Do not remember any other food.

Questioner: And what does *samrasi* mean?

Dadashri: *Samrasi* means to eat everything: sweet bread, soup, rice, vegetables. However, one should not indulge in sweet bread alone.

And some people give up eating sweet food. The sweet food will place a claim against them, "What have you got against me?" The fault is committed by one entity, but another gets punished! Hey, how can you punish the 'tongue' [taste buds]? The fault is of another entity. The fault lies with ignorance.

Questioner: But what is a *samrasi* diet? How can the same feeling be placed towards all food?

Dadashri: Whatever food is cooked in your culture, it is cooked based on what is considered *samrasi* for your culture. And when you serve that to somebody from another culture, they will not consider it *samrasi*. Perhaps in your culture, less spice is eaten. A *samrasi* diet is different for each culture. A *samrasi* diet means it is tasteful; tasty food. It means that no single ingredient dominates, all the ingredients are in proportion. Some people say, "I will get by with just drinking a glass of milk." That is not considered a *samrasi* diet. *Samrasi* means to combine all the six types of tastes together and then eat at ease, to eat it tastefully. If you cannot endure the bitter taste, then replace that by eating bitter gourd (*karela*), spine gourd (*kankoda*), or fenugreek leaves (*methi*) [all these have some degree of bitterness in them]; but you should definitely take in food that is bitter. Diseases arise as a result of not eating bitter foods. That is why you end up taking quinine [extremely bitter medicine to combat malaria]! It is indeed because there is a low intake of bitter taste that problems arise! There should be an intake of all six tastes.

Questioner: So it is for the intake of the tastes that we ask, "Oh Dada Bhagwan, give me the energy so that I take meals with a balance of all tastes."

Dadashri: Yes, you should ask for the energy. What is your intention? The intention to take in a *samrasi* diet is your effort [resolve towards that]. And as I give you the energy, that effort of yours becomes stronger!

Questioner: Is it also true that there should not be a prevalence in excessive temptation towards any taste?

Dadashri: Yes, so you should definitely not feel, 'I do not like any other food besides that with a sour taste.' Some people say, "I cannot do without something sweet." Then what fault is it of the spicy taste? Some people say, "I do not like sweet food at all. I only want spicy [food]." All that cannot be considered *samrasi*. *Samrasi* means that everything is accepted. It may be in a lesser or greater proportion, but everything is accepted.

Questioner: Is there any connection between Knowledge of the Self and a *samrasi* diet? For the awareness of the Knowledge, should we avoid meals that are not *samrasi*?

Dadashri: As far as a *samrasi* diet is concerned, for *mahatmas* (those who have received Knowledge of the Self), everything is subject to *vyavasthit* (scientific circumstantial evidences), so what is the need to fuss? This has been said for people at large [not Self-realized], however our *mahatmas* would at least think about eating as much of a *samrasi* diet as possible. I would say, "Bring me some chili peppers." And then I would also say, "I am taking medicine for cough!"

Then 'we' [the *Gnani Purush*] also Know when a remedy is given for the cough [arising out of eating spicy food]. This is because the [discharge] *prakruti* plays its part!

Multiplication and Division of the Prakruti

Questioner: So is it this *prakruti* that needs to have a *samrasi* diet?

Dadashri: What is the *prakruti*? When that which was multiplied by thirteen is divided by thirteen, that is when the *prakruti* comes to an end. Now what would happen when that which was multiplied by seventeen is divided by thirteen? Therefore, I have done a different calculation.

Questioner: So when that which was multiplied by thirteen, is divided by thirteen…

Dadashri: When you do that, there will be no remainder, right!

Questioner: In what way can we apply that example?

Dadashri: *Prakruti* means the intents (*bhaav*) that were done in the past life. Those intents were made on the basis of other food that was eaten. Now that intent has been multiplied by thirteen. If you now want to get rid of that intent, then if you divide it by thirteen, it will leave. And as a new intent is not allowed to arise, it means that account has been closed. There are no new desires, so the account closes. The account should be sealed.

…That Is Where the Prakruti Becomes Zero

Questioner: You have given us the Knowledge of the pure Soul. Now if we say these Nine *Kalams*, will they help bring the *prakruti* into the state of non-existence?

Dadashri: It will. Divide by however much you had multiplied. The doctor told me, "Eat this." I replied,

"Doctor, tell this to another patient. My 'multiplication' is of a different kind." How can it work out if he gives me the wrong figure to divide with?

Questioner: Are you then dividing it by sprinkling more red chili powder on your food?

Dadashri: While adding more red chili powder, I tell everyone that I am taking medicine for cough and when I get a cough, I point it out, 'Look, you got a cough, didn't you!'

Questioner: Where does the division come into this?

Dadashri: That itself is the division. If I hadn't taken the red pepper, then the division would not have been settled.

Questioner: So first, we are to clear off whatever has been filled in the *prakruti*.

Dadashri: Yes, it should be cleared off.

I tell Niruben, "If you agree, then I will have some *sopari* (betel nut, eaten as a mouth freshener)." But while chewing on the *sopari*, I say, "This is a medicine that causes cough." Many times she will say no, so I do not take it, and when she says yes, then I take it. Then I get a cough. However, it is not 'I' [Dada Bhagwan within] who eats the *sopari*. 'I' do not have a habit for anything. However, it is because the stock was filled in the past, that this [the act of eating *sopari*] happens, doesn't it?

This is our *Akram Vignan*! It is due to the habits that have been formed in the past life that this tends to happen. So ask for this energy. Then there is no problem with taking in food that is excessive [in one taste], but by saying this *Kalam*, the contracts [made in the past] get released.

Questioner: Whatever *prakruti* we have right now, if it is multiplied, then it will increase. It should be divided. 'The *prakruti* should be divided by the *prakruti*.' Please explain this.

Dadashri: So, when you keep saying these *Kalams*, the division will take place and it will decrease. If you do not say such *Kalams*, then the 'plant' will keep growing on its own. So if you keep saying this, then it will decrease. As you keep saying this, the multiplication of the *prakruti* that has taken place within, will be neutralized. The multiplication of the Self will take place and the division of the *prakruti* will take place. Therefore, the Self will get 'nourished'. If you have time, then keep saying these Nine *Kalams* day and night! The moment you get some free time, say them. 'We' give all the medicines, give the understanding, then whatever one wants to do...

For Those Present or Absent, Living or Dead...

Questioner: The eighth *Kalam*. "Oh Dada Bhagwan, give me the absolute energy not to, nor cause anyone to, nor instigate anyone to criticize, offend, or disrespect any being, be they present or absent, living or dead."

Dadashri: *Avarnavaad* means that if someone has a good reputation, he is well-respected, he is renowned, yet we speak ill of him and break that reputation down, that is referred to as *avarnavaad*. To denigrate him.

Questioner: In reference to that, when we ask for forgiveness from those who are dead, whatever we address to them, does that actually reach them?

Dadashri: You do not have to make it reach them. You will incur a tremendous fault if you curse a person who is no longer living. That is what this *Kalam* is conveying. That is why I am telling you to not speak against even those who are dead. As such, there is no question of it reaching or not reaching the person. Say there is a corrupt person who did evil things during his lifetime, even then we should not speak ill of him after he has passed away.

At present, you should not speak ill about Raavan (Lord Rama's adversary in the epic *Ramayana*), because he is still in the physical form somewhere. So the 'phone call' reaches him. When you say, "Raavan was like this and like that," it reaches him.

If people are backbiting about a dead relative of yours, then you must not get involved in that. If you happen to become involved in it, then you should later repent that, 'This should not happen.' It is a tremendous offence to speak ill about a person who is dead. Our folks do not even leave the dead alone. Do people not do that? This should not be so; that is what 'we' are conveying. There is grave liability in that.

One may perhaps end up speaking thus based on opinions of the past. If you simultaneously recite this *Kalam*, then when you end up speaking in that way, you will not incur a fault. While smoking a hookah, if you keep saying, "Give me the energy to not smoke, nor cause anyone to smoke, nor instigate anyone to smoke," then the contracts made in the past get released. Otherwise, the inherent nature of the *pudgal* (non-Self complex) is to lead you astray. That is why these intentions should be nurtured.

Grant the Energy to Become an Instrument for World Salvation

Questioner: The ninth *Kalam*. "Oh Dada Bhagwan, give me the absolute energy to become an instrument for the salvation of the world." If we nurture this intention for world salvation, then how does it work?

Dadashri: Your words will come forth such that the other person's work will be done.

Questioner: Are you referring to salvation in the relative sense [materialistic; for the non-Self complex] or of the Real [of the Self]?

Dadashri: Not of the relative, we only need that which takes us towards the Real. Then with the aid of the Real, there will be progress [in the relative]. If you attain the Real, then you will definitely attain the relative! Develop the intention for the salvation of the entire world. You should not say it just for the sake of saying it; nurture the intention. People just recite it for the sake of reciting it, just as if they are reciting holy chants.

Questioner: Instead of just sitting idly, it would be considered best to nurture such an intention, wouldn't it?

Dadashri: That is very good. At least the negative intents are destroyed! From this intention, however much you are able to nurture, that much is good; you have gained that much at least!

Questioner: Can this intention be considered a mechanical intention?

Dadashri: No. How can it be considered mechanical? It is mechanical when one keeps repeating it excessively and meaninglessly. If one keeps saying it without it remaining in one's awareness, then it is mechanical!

Nothing Actually Needs To Be Done in This

Questioner: It is written in the Nine *Kalams*, 'Give me the energy, give me the energy.' So, do we get the energy just by reading that?

Dadashri: Definitely! These are the words of the *Gnani Purush* (one who has experienced the Self and is able to do the same for others)! Is there not a difference between a letter from the Prime Minister and a letter from a merchant? Why are you not responding? Yes, so these are the words of the *Gnani Purush*. If a person tries to understand this using his intellect, then it will not do. These are things that are beyond the intellect.

Questioner: But in order to bring it into effect, I will have to do what is written in here, won't I?

Dadashri: No, this is only to be read. It will come into effect on its own. So you should keep this book with you all the time and read it daily. You will learn all of the knowledge that is in here. As you continue to read it daily, it will come into practice. You will become that form. It will not be so evident today, the benefit you have gotten out of this! But gradually, it will become exact for you.

The result of asking for this energy is that it will definitely come into conduct, eventually. So you should ask for the energies from Dada Bhagwan. And Dada Bhagwan has unlimited, infinite energies, the kind which will give you whatever you ask for! So by asking for this energy, what will happen?

Questioner: The energy will be attained!

Dadashri: Yes, the energy to follow these [*Kalams*] will arise, and thereafter, you will be able to abide by them. You cannot abide by them just like that. Therefore, you should keep asking for the energy. You do not have to do anything else. Conduct such as that which is written [in the Nine *Kalams*] cannot happen immediately, and it will not happen either. 'You' [the Self] simply have to Know however much you ['Chandubhai'] are able to do and ask for forgiveness for however much you are not able to do. And along with that, ask for this energy, so you will get the energy.

Accomplish Your Work By Asking for the Energy

I told a man, "Everything is encompassed in these Nine *Kalams*. Nothing has been left out in this. Read these Nine *Kalams* every day!" To which he replied, "But this cannot be done." So I said, "I am not telling you to do anything." Why are you saying that it cannot be done? All you have to say is, "Oh Dada Bhagwan, give me the energy." I am telling you to ask for the energy. Then he replied, "This will actually be fun!" People have actually taught us to 'do' things [to improve our behavior].

Then he asked me, "Who will give this energy?" I said, "I will give the energies." I am ready to give the energies you ask for. As you yourself do not know how to ask, I have to teach you to ask in this way, don't I? Just look, haven't I taught you all this! These are indeed things I have taught you, aren't they? So he understood. Then he said, "This much can be done, everything is encompassed in this."

You do not have to do this. Do not do anything at all. Eat two more *rotlis* (Indian flat bread) than you normally eat, but ask for this energy. Then he said to me, "I like this point."

Questioner: Initially, there is this very doubt, 'Will I get the energy if I ask for it or not?'

Dadashri: That very doubt will prove to be wrong. Now you are asking for that energy, aren't you! So once that energy arises within, then that energy itself will ensure that the work gets carried out. 'You' [the Self] do not have to do anything. If you attempt to do anything, then the egoism will increase. You will say, "I am trying my best to do it, but it is not happening." So just ask for the energy.

Questioner: In these Nine *Kalams*, when we ask for energy not to do, nor cause anyone to do, nor instigate anyone to do, then does that mean that we are asking for the energy so that it will not happen in the future or is it to wash off our past deeds?

Dadashri: The past deeds get washed off and the energies arise. The energies are already there, but by washing those off, the energies manifest. The energies are already there, but they have to manifest. That is why we ask for the grace of Dada Bhagwan, "If this of ours gets washed off, then the energies will manifest."

Questioner: I read all this; this is actually a phenomenal discussion. If even an ordinary person understands this, then his entire life will pass by in happiness.

Dadashri: Yes, otherwise he had not found anything that was worth understanding [until now]. This is the first time that he is getting something that is clearly worth understanding. Now, once he gets that, the solution will come about.

Of these Nine *Kalams*, there is no problem with following as many as you are able to of your own accord. But if you are not able to follow them, then there is no need to feel regret for that in your mind. All you have to do is to ask for the energy. That energy will keep accumulating. The energy will keep getting deposited within. Then the work will get done automatically. In fact, all of the Nine *Kalams* will be set up the moment you ask for the energy! So it is enough even if you just say them. If you say them, it means you asked for the energy, and so you will get the energy.

Purification of Intent Through These Intentions

Questioner: You said that although one may be smoking hookah, but what is going on from within is, 'to not smoke, nor cause anyone to smoke, nor instigate anyone to smoke...'

Dadashri: Yes, all that means to say is, 'You do not agree with this'; that is what 'we' are trying to convey. It means that your opinion differs from the action. And when the hookah goes away on its own, then it will be legitimate. So now, you are no longer stuck to it, it is stuck to you. What I am trying to say is that when its duration is over, it will go away. If on one hand, one smokes the hookah, and on the other hand, he declares this intention, then the [liability for] smoking vanishes, and this intention has begun [to come into effect].

When you go unannounced to someone's house, the person may say, "Come sir, come sir," but from within he may feel, 'Why did he have to come right now?' It means that he is saying the opposite of what is going on in his mind. On the outside, he says, "Welcome," but then again from within he says, 'Why now?' So, he is spoiling that which is already good. Whereas what does the former situation convey? One smokes the hookah, but [from within he says,] 'This should not be so.' So here, we are improving that which is spoiled.

Questioner: The most astonishing thing of the entire *Akram Vignan* is that it is spoiled on the outside and it is being improved on the inside.

Dadashri: Yes, that is why we feel satisfied, isn't it! It does not matter if the current 'situation' [life] is spoiled, but the new one will definitely be better. That which is ruined is history, but at least the new one will be better, won't it? Whereas some people keep saying, "We only want to improve this life." Hey, let it go. Just let go of it, from here. The next one will become spoiled as well. You will incur a double loss.

Questioner: We are not currently responsible for that which is spoiled right now. That is a result of the past life.

Dadashri: Yes, we are not responsible right now. That power lies in the hands of another entity right now. It is beyond your control! This is actually not going to change, so why do you needlessly become restless! Yet even the religious teacher will say, "If you can't do this, then you will not be allowed to enter." His follower will respond, "But sir, I really want to do this, but I am not able to. So what can I do?" Such rampant misunderstanding prevails.

Questioner: When the *prakruti* (non-Self complex) causes a lot of havoc, then one feels tremendous suffocation within.

Dadashri: Oh, when such a thing happens, then he does not eat for five days. Alas, who is at fault and who is getting the beating for it! Why are you punishing the stomach? The fault is of the mind and he punishes the stomach. He will say, "You will not get to eat." What can the poor man do? His energy will diminish, won't it! If he has eaten, then he may be able to do some other work. That is why our people say, "Why are you punishing someone for a fault committed by another?' The fault is of the mind, what fault is it of the poor body?

Moreover, what will one gain out of clearing away the external? That which we have no control over whatsoever! What is the point of needlessly screaming and shouting? The rubbish within will have to be swept away. Everything on the inside has to be cleansed. Instead, people cleanse the external. When they go in the river Ganges, they keep submerging their bodies. Hey, of what use is it to wash off the body? Why don't you wash off the mind! The mind, the intellect, the *chit* (subtle component of vision and knowledge), the ego, all of them, the *antahkaran* (internal functioning mechanism in every human being composed of the mind, intellect, *chit* and ego) has to be washed off. Soap has never even been used on these, so then won't they become soiled?

Everything is fine as long as one is of a young age.

Then with each day, things become soiled and thereafter, rubbish gathers about. That is why I say, "Leave your conduct outside and take this along with you. Leave all these lies outside and nurture these *Kalams*, then your next life will be topmost!

Questioner: People who have not taken this Knowledge of the Self can also change their behavior in this manner, can't they?

Dadashri: Yes, they can change everything. Everyone has the liberty to recite these *Kalams*.

Questioner: When something bad happens, these *Kalams* are a potent solution to wash it off.

Dadashri: This is actually a great *purusharth* (effort to progress on the path of liberation). So 'we' have disclosed this, the greatest science of all. However, people must now understand it! That is why I have made it mandatory to do this much. Even if you don't understand it, just drink this 'medicine' [Nine *Kalams*]!

Questioner: The internal diseases will be destroyed.

Dadashri: Yes, they will be destroyed. Dada has said to read this, so just read it. That is more than enough! This is not meant to be digested. This is like dissolving a tablet and drinking it and then going about your business confidently!

Questioner: Is it true that one's spiritual worthiness (*patrata*) can be increased by maintaining the intent (*bhaav*)?

Dadashri: The real *purusharth* is verily the intent. All these other concepts are baseless. The state of doership is a state of bondage, whereas this intent [as the Self, of non-doership] is a state that leads to liberation. People have become bound by, 'Do this, do that, do such and such,' haven't they!

The Intention Will Give Effect in the Next Life

Questioner: When an incident happens where I end up hurting someone's ego, in that instance, can I recite that *Kalam*, '...to not hurt the ego of any living being...'?

Dadashri: At that time, You should tell 'Chandubhai', 'Do *pratikraman* for the hurt you have caused him.' And do not make a fuss about other small matters. Anyways, one generally does not have traits so intense that they would cause anyone's ego to be hurt. And if the situation is such that someone is hurt slightly, then make him ['Chandubhai'] do *pratikraman* for it.

Actually, these intentions are to be nurtured. One lifetime still remains [until liberation], so this intention will give effect. At that time [in the next life], you will have become the very form of these intentions. Your conduct will be exactly as is written in these intentions, but in the next life! At present, the seeds have been sown, so it will not do if you were to say right now, "Come, let's dig them up and eat them."

Questioner: The effect will not come in this life, it will come in the next life?

Dadashri: Yes, one to two lives still remain. That is why we are sowing these seeds, so that everything will be clear in the next life. This is for those who want to sow the seeds.

Questioner: So should we recite these constantly, meaning as and when an incident arises?

Dadashri: No, that incident and nurturing these intentions have nothing to do with each other. What does the incident have to do with this? The incident is without any basis! Whereas these intentions are something with a basis. These intentions will accompany You into your next life, whereas the incident will come to an end.

Questioner: But isn't it on the basis of an incident that we are able to nurture these intentions?

Dadashri: No. Incidents have nothing to do with it. Only the intentions will carry forward with You. The incident is without any basis, it will disperse. No matter how wonderful the incident, it too will pass. This is because it is a circumstance that has arisen, and these intentions are to be nurtured. Their circumstances are yet to be formed.

Questioner: But it is due to these incidents that our intent changes; isn't that when we are to use this intention and turn the intent back around?

Dadashri: But it is not as if it helps. Whatever had been done in the past [life], that much will help right now. Yes, it is possible if you had started this process in your previous life, only then would it turn around completely in this life.

Questioner: So, in the case of incidents, if the intents were there in the past life, do only those come into effect right now?

Dadashri: Only those will come into effect. Nothing else will come. *Bhaav* (intent) is the seed, and *dravya* (that which unfolds as events in this life) is the effect, the crop. Just one millet seed is sown, yet it gives rise to many more!

These *Kalams* are simply to be spoken. The intention just needs to be nurtured daily. The seed is to be planted. After planting it, watch the effect when it comes forth. Until then, provide the fertilizer. Otherwise, there is nothing that needs to be turned around in these incidents. And whatever is unfolding now, it is only that which has been carried over from the past [life].

So what do these Nine *Kalams* say? "Oh Dada Bhagwan, give me the energy." Now what do people say? "It is not possible to abide by them." But this is not something to be done. Hey, why are you acting crazy! Everyone in this world has said, "Do this, do this, do this." Hey, there is nothing to be done; One only has to Know. And then ask Dada Bhagwan for forgiveness in this way, "I do not want to do this, and I am repenting for it." Now, from the moment you say, "I do not want to do this," from that moment onwards, your opinion becomes different [from the action]. Then even if you do that thing, there is no problem with it. But because the opinion became different [from the action], you are free [from the liability]! This is the secret of the path of liberation; the world is not aware of it!

Questioner: Are they only striving for changes in the discharge [part]; are these people striving to make changes in the effect?

Dadashri: Yes, therefore the world does not know of this attentive awareness at all, they have no clue at all. I am trying to free people of their opinions. Right now, 'This is wrong,' such is the opinion that has been established within you. This is because, before, there was the opinion that 'This is right', and worldly life perpetuated through that. And now, as the opinion forms that, 'This is wrong,' you become free. Now this opinion should not change again under any circumstance!

If you say these Nine *Kalams* every day, then gradually there will be no fighting or conflicts with anyone. This is because Your own intent [as the Self] no longer remains engrossed in the non-Self complex. Now all that remains is that which is reactionary. That will gradually keep decreasing.

Is It Charge or Discharge for Mahatmas?

Questioner: What is the difference between *bhaav* and *bhaavna*?

Dadashri: They both fall under 'Chandubhai'! But it is true, there is a difference between *bhaav* and *bhaavna*.

Questioner: *Bhaavna* is pure (*pavitra*) and *bhaav* can be either good or bad.

Dadashri: No, it is not that *bhaavna* is pure. *Bhaavna* is applicable even to the impure (*apavitra*). One may even have the *bhaavna* of burning down someone's house, and one may even have the *bhaavna* of building a house for someone. So *bhaavna* can be used for both sides, but *bhaav* is considered charge and *bhaavna* is discharge.

When you feel, 'I have a *bhaav* to do this, I have to do it this way,' that too is a *bhaavna*, it is not *bhaav*. Truly speaking, *bhaav* is only that which is charge.

So, this world has come into existence due to *bhaavkarma* (subtle charge karma). Even if you cannot do a certain thing, you must still maintain a *bhaav* to do it. I have done away with *bhaav* for you [*mahatmas*]. For people who are not Self-realized, they should do *bhaavkarma*. As in, they should ask for the energy. Whatever energy they want, they should ask for that from Dada Bhagwan.

Questioner: People [not Self-realized] out there in the world should ask for this energy. So the energy that our *mahatmas* ask for, the *bhaavna* that they do, what does that fall under?

Dadashri: What *mahatmas* ask for falls under discharge. This is because there are two types of *bhaavna*, charge and discharge. People out there in worldly interaction [not Self-realized] also have *bhaavna*, and we too have *bhaavna* here. But ours is in the form of discharge and theirs is in the form of both, charge and discharge. But what is the harm in asking for the energy?

Questioner: When people out there [not Self-realized]

ask for the energy in these Nine *Kalams*, then it is considered *bhaav*. But when *mahatmas* ask for the energy, is that not considered *bhaav*?

Dadashri: For people out there [not Self-realized], it is considered *bhaav* and for our *mahatmas*, it is *bhaavna*. That is true. Those *bhaav* are considered as charge. And this [*bhaavna*] is considered as discharge, it cannot be called *bhaav*!

Bhaav, Exactly in Accordance With the Design

Questioner: Our *bhaavna*, desire, everything, even opinions, are only in accordance with what is in these Nine *Kalams*, just as these Nine *Kalams* say.

Dadashri: It may appear as if one is doing the same as he was before, but it is not exactly the same. It is decided that there is an inclination (*valan*) on this side, but that inclination should definitely be of this type. It should be in accordance with the design. There may be an inclination, there indeed may be the desire not to harass monks and ascetics! But it should be in accordance with the design.

Questioner: In what way do you mean, 'It should be in accordance with the design,' Dada?

Dadashri: It should be in accordance with what is written in there [in the Nine *Kalams*], in exactness. Otherwise, it is generally the norm that people do not want to hurt any monk or saint, but they still end up doing so. What is the reason for this? It is because theirs is not in accordance with the design. If it were in accordance with the design, then this would not happen.

Questioner: Should these Nine *Kalams* be incorporated into our lives with understanding?

Dadashri: No, it does not need to be incorporated into life with understanding. What I am conveying is, just ask for the energy that I have spoken about here. That will bring it into exactness for you. You do not have to do it with understanding. That won't ever happen, a person cannot do such a thing. If someone attempts to do it with understanding, then it won't happen. Leave it in the hands of nature. Which means to say, "Dada Bhagwan, give me the energy." The energy will arise by itself. Then it will come in exactness.

This is a very elevated thing. Until it is understood, it carries on like this!

Why would I have said, "Ask for the energy, please give me the energy"? It is because one cannot make the design himself. How can he make the original design? Therefore, this is an effect. The energy you ask for is the cause and that which will come forth is the effect. Through whom does this effect come? It has been facilitated through Dada Bhagwan. The effect should come through the Lord.

So if one keeps asking for the energy according to the Nine *Kalams*, then after many years, he will prevail in the Nine *Kalams* automatically.

In Order to Become Free From Worldly Relations...

Questioner: These Nine *Kalams* have indeed been given for the purification of thought, speech, and action, haven't they?

Dadashri: No, no. There is no need for that here. There is no need for that on the *Akram* path. These Nine *Kalams* have been given to release you from the karmic accounts that have been bound from infinite past lives. They have been given to clear your karmic ledger.

So if you say the Nine *Kalams*, then the link will break. The link that has been created with people, that *roonanubandh* (karmic ties created through attachment-abhorrence in the past life) does not allow you to become liberated. So these Nine *Kalams* are for breaking those links.

By saying these [Nine *Kalams*], all the mistakes you have made up until now will become a little lax [not so tightly bound]. And actually, their effect will definitely come forth later. They become like a cindered rope, so when you touch it with your hand, it will disintegrate.

Questioner: If I keep on saying the Nine *Kalams* in order to do *pratikraman* for my faults, then is there really energy in that?

Dadashri: The Nine *Kalams* that you say are different and the *pratikraman* you do for your faults is different. You should do *pratikraman* daily for whatever faults that arise.

In fact, by saying the Nine *Kalams*, the discord that has occurred over the course of infinite past lives, all the karmic ties get released. It is *pratikraman*, it is the greatest *pratikraman*. The *pratikraman* of the entire world is incorporated in these Nine *Kalams*. Do it properly. Having shown this to you, I am done with my work. Then I will move on to my realm [the final destination]!

Dada Prevailed in the Nine Kalams Throughout His Life

It is due to the current era of the time cycle that people do not have the energy. I have given you only this much to ask for, only these energies that have been listed here. If one nurtures these intentions, then I can guarantee that they will not lose the life-form as a human being in their next life. Otherwise, eighty percent of the current human population will not retain their life-form as a human being. Such are the times.

These Nine *Kalams* contain the highest of intentions. The entire essence is captured in them. I have been practicing these Nine *Kalams* my entire life; they are in fact my wealth. So, I have disclosed my daily practices. This is ultimately for the sake of the salvation of the public. These Nine *Kalams* have been going on within daily, constantly, for so many years, for the past forty years. I now present them to the public.

Questioner: Right now, we say, "Oh Dada Bhagwan, give me the energy." So, whom did you refer to when you said these Nine *Kalams*?

Dadashri: It may not have been Dada Bhagwan, there may have been some other name, but there was definitely a name. I would say them referring only to Him. You can call Him pure Soul or whatever else, but I would say them referring only to Him.

On the *Kramik* path (traditional step-by-step path of spiritual progress), one reads voluminous scriptures, whereas here [in *Akram*], it is more than enough to just say these Nine *Kalams*! So much energy has been placed in the Nine *Kalams*. There is tremendous energy, but it is not easily understood! It is only when I explain it, that it is understood. The person who comes to me and tells me, "I really like these Nine *Kalams*," has actually understood their value. And these Nine *Kalams* are worth understanding.

These Nine *Kalams* are not in the scriptures. But what 'we' [the *Gnani Purush*] abide by and is always in 'our' application is what 'we' have given you to do. These *Kalams* have been written according to the way 'we' prevail. 'Our' conduct is in accordance with the Nine *Kalams*, nevertheless, 'we' are not considered God (*Bhagwan*). God is verily the One who resides within! Besides, a person cannot conduct himself in this manner.

The essence of the fourteen worlds is captured in just this much. These Nine *Kalams* that have been written are the essence of the fourteen worlds. It is as though I have taken out the butter and placed it here, after having churned the yogurt of all these fourteen worlds. What tremendous merit *karma* all these people have; they are headed towards liberation while standing in an elevator! Yes, the only condition is, do not stick your hand outside!

These Nine *Kalams* are not to be found anywhere else. Only the fully enlightened One (*purna Purush*) can write the Nine *Kalams*. Such a person is very rare! If He is present, then people will attain salvation.

The Essence of the Science of Liberation!

And when these intentions are being done, how should it be? While reading them, each and every word should be seen. If You can See that 'Chandubhai' is reading them, then You are not entangled elsewhere. 'You' should not be lost elsewhere whilst nurturing these intentions. 'We' do not go anywhere else even for a moment. 'You' too will have to get on that path, won't you? At the very place that 'we' are at! The moment these intentions are nurtured, One begins to become complete (*purna*). It is worth doing only these intentions.

Yes, speak these intentions with the unity of the mind, speech, and body. So definitely do these Nine *Kalams* from now on. These Nine *Kalams* are the essence of the entire science of liberation (*Vitaraag Vignan*)! And *pratikraman* and *pratyakhyan* (avowal to not repeat a mistake); all that is encompassed within this. Such *Kalams* have not been published anywhere else. Just as the book on *brahmacharya* (absolute celibacy through the mind, speech, and body) has not been published anywhere else, these *Kalams* too have not been published anywhere else. If a person reads the Nine *Kalams*, if he nurtures these intentions, then he will not have vengeance with anyone in this world. There will be friendship with everyone! These Nine *Kalams* are the essence of all the scriptures!

Jai Sat Chit Anand
(Awareness of the Eternal is Bliss)

Spiritual Glossary

Gujarati Word	English Translation
abhaav	dislike
Akram Vignan	the spiritual science of the step-less path to Self-realization
aparaadh	to intentionally oppose another living being
avarnavaad	to not depict something as it is by any means possible, but to depict the opposite; to say that which is not fact
avinay	disrespect; lack of humility
bhaav	intent
bhaav pratikraman	reversal of aggression in thoughts, speech and action by changing the inner intent
bhaavkarma	subtle charge karma
bhaavna	intention
cheshtao	actions of the body that can be photographed; gestures
dharma	religion; function
Gnan	Knowledge of the Self
Gnani Purush	One who has realized the Self and is able to do the same for others
jagruti	awareness
lubdhapanu	to prevail in excessive temptation
mahatmas	Self-realized ones in *Akram Vignan*
mrudu	with humility
nimit	One who is instrumental in a process
ninda	backbiting
Nine Kalams (Nav Kalamo)	nine statements in which one asks for energy to the pure Soul within for the highest spiritual intents

prakruti	mind-speech-body complex
pramaan	foundation of one's belief system
pratikraman	exact method of reversal from aggression through confession of a mistake, apology, and resolution not to repeat the mistake
purusharth	effort to progress on the path of liberation
ruju	straightforward
sampurna	complete
samrasi	balance of all six tastes
shakti	energy
siddhi	spiritual power
syadvaad	that which is accepted by all and does not hurt anyone's viewpoint; to accept the foundation of each person's belief system
syadvaad vani	speech that is accepted by all
tantilli	hurtful
tiraskaar	contempt
Tirthankar	the absolutely enlightened Lord who can liberate others
varnavaad	to say something as it is
viradhana	to speak that which is contrary to fact about a person, leading to spiritual descent
vitaraag	free from attachment and abhorrence

❖ ❖ ❖ ❖ ❖

Contacts

Dada Bhagwan Foundation

India :

Adalaj (Main Center)	:	**Trimandir**, Simandhar City, Ahmedabad-Kalol Highway, Adalaj, Dist.: Gandhinagar - 382421, Gujarat, India. **Tel :** + 91 79 35002100, +91 9328661166-77 **Email :** info@dadabhagwan.org
Bangalore	:	+91 95909 79099
Delhi	:	+91 98100 98564
Kolkata	:	+91 98300 93230
Mumbai	:	+91 93235 28901

Other Countries :

Argentina	:	**Tel:** +54 91158431163 **Email:** info@dadabhagwan.ar
Australia	:	**Tel:** +61 402179706 **Email:** sydney@au.dadabhagwan.org
Brazil	:	**Tel:** +55 11999828971 **Email:** info@br.dadabhagwan.org
Germany	:	**Tel:** +49 700 DADASHRI (32327474) **Email:** info@dadabhagwan.de
Kenya	:	**Tel:** +254 79592 DADA (3232) **Email:** info@ke.dadabhagwan.org
New Zealand	:	**Tel:** +64 21 0376434 **Email:** info@nz.dadabhagwan.org
Singapore	:	**Tel:** + 65 91457800 **Email:** info@sg.dadabhagwan.org
Spain	:	**Tel:** +34 922302706 **Email:** info@dadabhagwan.es
UAE	:	**Tel:** +971 557316937 **Email:** dubai@ae.dadabhagwan.org
UK	:	**Tel :** +44 330-111-DADA (3232) **Email :** info@uk.dadabhagwan.org
USA-Canada	:	**Tel :** +1 877-505-DADA (3232) **Email :** info@us.dadabhagwan.org

Website : www.dadabhagwan.org